The
Irish Narrow Gauge
Railway

J. D. C. A. Prideaux

DAVID & CHARLES
Newton Abbot   London   North Pomfret (Vt)

© Dr J. D. C. A. Prideaux 1981

British Library Cataloguing in Publication Data

Prideaux, J. D. C. A.
  The Irish narrow gauge railway.
  1. Railroads, narrow gauge – Ireland – History
  I. Title
  385′.52′094169   HE3828

Photoset by
Northern Phototypesetting Co., Bolton
and printed in Great Britain
by Biddles Ltd., Guildford, Surrey
for David & Charles (Publishers) Limited
Brunel House, Newton Abbot, Devon

Published in the United States of America
by David & Charles Inc.
North Pomfret Vermont 05053 USA

0715380710

Front cover: Cork & Muskerry 4–4–0T No 7 *Peake* heads
seven coaches and two vans along Western Road, Cork
around 1900. (*L&GRP*).

Back cover: County Donegal 4–6–4T No 10 *Owena* leaves
Strabane for Stranolar in May 1937. (*R. G. Jarvis*).

CONTENTS

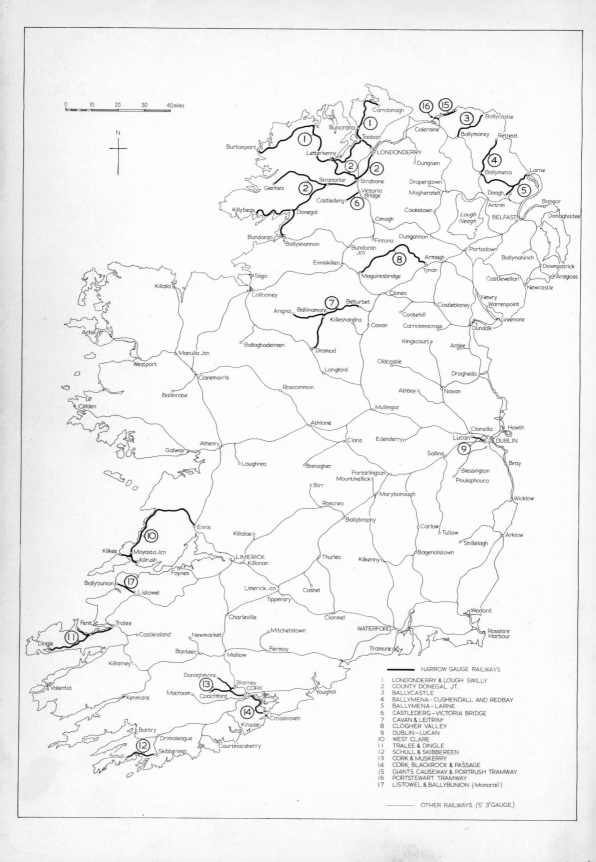

NARROW GAUGE RAILWAYS

1 LONDONDERRY & LOUGH SWILLY
2 COUNTY DONEGAL JT.
3 BALLYCASTLE
4 BALLYMENA—CUSHENDALL AND REDBAY
5 BALLYMENA—LARNE
6 CASTLEDERG—VICTORIA BRIDGE
7 CAVAN & LEITRIM
8 CLOGHER VALLEY
9 DUBLIN—LUCAN
10 WEST CLARE
11 TRALEE & DINGLE
12 SCHULL & SKIBBEREEN
13 CORK & MUSKERRY
14 CORK, BLACKROCK & PASSAGE
15 GIANTS CAUSEWAY & PORTRUSH TRAMWAY
16 PORTSTEWART TRAMWAY
17 LISTOWEL & BALLYBUNION (Monorail)

——— OTHER RAILWAYS (5' 3" GAUGE)

INTRODUCTION

The narrow gauge represented over 15 per cent of the Irish railway network. About 570 miles were built, more than twice the narrow gauge mileage of the rest of the British Isles put together. These railways were (with one exception) built to a 3ft gauge. There was variety in just about everything other than gauge: traction was generally by steam, but occasionally by horse or electricity, loading gauges were different on each line, coupling arrangements were not standardised and even where lines joined through working of stock of trains could be complicated by such a simple matter as different fastenings on the vacuum brake hoses. As for locomotives and rolling stock, practically every line was different.

The railways were generally rural. In this they reflected the nature of most of the country. They had no part in the growth of Belfast as an industrial city. One line ran from Dublin itself, and several connected such cities as Cork and Londonderry with their hinterland. Passenger traffic on such lines included many excursionists, as well as people persuing the more basic rural need to travel to market towns; regrettably also there were many one-way tickets for rural Irish men and women who had decided that the future lay abroad. Freight was very mixed. Livestock was important, hardly suprising in a pastoral country. Guinness (and other drinks), and fish also feature fairly regularly in the list of traffics. Coal, the cornerstone of any English railway's freight receipts was however less important in Ireland where the rural community largely depended on local peat for fuel.

The first Irish narrow gauge lines were built in County Antrim. There is a substantial amount of iron ore north-east of Ballymena. The first line, the Ballymena, Cushendall & Red Bay Railway received the royal assent on 18 July 1872. It was authorised to build a railway to any gauge the company saw fit provided it was between two and three feet. As the 3ft gauge was recommended at that time by Spooner, who had established a world wide reputation as a result of the work carried out on the Festiniog Railway in Wales, it is not suprising that this gauge was adopted. The $16\frac{1}{2}$ miles of railway opened in 1875, but at that stage was purely a goods line carrying iron ore. At much the same time a similar line four miles in length was opened connecting the lower part of Glenariff to a pier. Unfortunately the supply of iron ore was not as large as had been hoped and during the 1880s cheaper and richer ore increasingly supplanted it in English furnaces. However the introduction of the narrow gauge railway had provided the stimulus and the first section of the Ballymena & Larne Railway opened in 1878. The object of this line was to connect Ballymena with Larne for general traffic and to provide an outlet to the sea for the iron ore coming off the Cushendall line. The Ballymena & Larne was the first Irish narrow gauge line to provide for all classes of traffic.

By the end of the 1870s some 45 miles of railway had been built to a gauge adopted almost by accident. The 1880s were to prove the most vigorous years of expansion. In all, just over 250 miles or 45 per cent of the total Irish narrow gauge network opened at this time. A substantial number of lines followed the previous procedure of private funding and construction under an individual Act of Parliament. The first of these was the Ballycastle running from Ballymoney, some way to the north of Ballymena but still in County Antrim (1880). The early 1880s saw the first narrow gauge sections of what were to become the largest networks, those of the Donegal (1882) and Lough Swilly (1883). Several roadside tramways also opened at much the same time, the Portstewart tramway (1882), the first section of the Dublin & Lucan Railway (1881), the Giant's Causeway and the Castlederg & Victoria Bridge tramway (both 1883). The Giant's Causeway was remarkable in that it used a mixture of steam and electric working. All these railways were built by private companies using their own Acts. The last such railway to open a new line in the 1880s was the Listowel & Ballybunion (1888). This was the one railway which did not use the standard 3ft gauge. It was built using the Lartigue monorail system, very much in the hope that it would be adopted by other light railway promoters. As a demonstration it seems primarily to have succeeded in convincing people of the disadvantages of monorails!

The Tramways & Public Expenses (Ireland) Act was passed in 1883. Under its provisions, the promoters of a public tramway company could apply to the Grand Jury (the precursor of the modern county council) which could require that the Baronies (district councils) guarantee part or all of the capital of the line. Thus in essence the promoter could establish a position where his returns were guaranteed. This hardly made for efficient control of the railways, particularly as interest was normally guaranteed at 5 per cent which was rather above what most Irish railway companies managed to pay. The Treasury would refund part of the Baronies' contribution but nevertheless the unfortunate Baronies could be landed with a substantial bill for support. While the principle that where a local community wanted to see communications improved it should contribute towards it was undoubtedly fair, the manner in which it was implemented in this Act was far from ideal. Six complete railway systems were built under the Act, which also enabled the West Donegal to complete its line to Donegal town. The first was the Schull & Skibbereen in 1886. It was inadequately built and seriously under-equipped. Services even had to be suspended for nine months shortly after opening, to allow matters to be sorted out. Fortunately, the promoters of most of the other railways built under the Act did not show quite such indifference. In 1887 the first sections of four other railways opened. These were the Cavan & Leitrim, Clogher Valley, the Cork & Muskerry Light and the West Clare. The last railway built under the Act was the Tralee & Dingle, which opened in 1891. It managed to rival the Schull & Skibbereen for its financial and railway operating peccadilloes.

The financial inadequacies of the 1883 Act were immediately evident. They were severely criticised by the Allport Commission in the middle 1880s. Subsequent Acts put the initiative for a new railway, if it were to be substantially supported by public funds, directly on the Government. Under the 1889 Act the Lord Lieutenant of Ireland could declare that a light railway was needed for the development of fisheries or other industries and make available grants or loans for construction and (if necessary) to contribute towards working costs. The railways had to be worked by an existing company in the hope that this would get round the worst of the management failures of the 1883 Act. In result, this Act was very similar to a subsequent Act of 1896. Each Act resulted in two railways being built in Donegal. The parts of Donegal concerned were classed as congested. The official definition of congested was that the annual rateable value per head was less than thirty shillings. A contemporary Government report was more evocative: 'In the congested districts there are two classes, namely the poor and the destitute'. The Congested Districts Board sought the expansion of the coastal fishing industry and the provision of transport to give the fish access to market. The two lines built under the 1889 Act were extensions of the Donegal system. This lead to the railway reaching Killybegs in 1893 and Glenties in 1895. The two railways built under the 1896 Act were extensions of the Lough Swilly Railway. The railway opened from Buncrana to Carndonagh in 1901, and from Letterkenny to Burtonport (a distance of nearly 50 miles) in 1903. In total the railways built under these two Acts on Government initiative represented something like 20 per cent of the Irish narrow gauge system.

All this Government assistance to provide railways for the less fortunate districts did not prevent further expansion under private Acts. Three railways which had been built to the Irish 5ft 3in gauge were converted to the 3ft gauge when they extended. The first of these was the Lough Swilly in 1885, a sensible provision since that railway was already working the Letterkenny line on the narrow gauge. Something very similar happened to the Finn Valley railway, part of the Donegal system in 1894. The final example of gauge conversion occurred in 1900 when the Cork, Blackrock & Passage converted its line to the 3ft gauge as a preliminary for extension to Crosshaven. Completely new railways were also opened under private Acts in the first years of this century. All were extensions of the Donegal system which built from Strabane to Londonderry in 1900, from Donegal to Ballyshannon in 1905 and finally (through a nominally private company) from Strabane to Letterkenny in 1909. This was the last substantial stretch of Irish narrow gauge railway to open, although a short extension from the Cavan & Leitrim to Arigna coal mines opened under provisions of the Defence of the Realm Act in 1920.

The heyday of the Irish narrow gauge railway came to an abrupt end with the first world war.

A passenger train on the Cushendall line. Belfast &
Northern Counties Railway 0—4—2 ST No 60 at Ballymena.
(*Leabharlann Naisiunta na hEireann*).

Government control was imposed in 1916 and
costs (particularly fuel and wages) rose by 250 per
cent to 1921. While fares and other receipts were
slowly increased they did not keep pace with the
rise in costs. The end of the first world war found
Ireland an unsettled place, with conflict between
British forces and those supporting independence
developing from 1920. None of the railways
escaped incident and those in some parts of the
west were very badly affected indeed.
Occasionally the political aspects had their
humourous or ridiculous sides. In 1920 and 1921
the Cavan & Leitrim was not paid the monies due
from Leitrim Council under the Baronial
guarantee, because the council had withdrawn its
recognition of the British Government and thus
could not reclaim the proportion unwritten by an
unrecognised Treasury. And a Mr Stack was
appointed Chairman of the Tralee & Dingle by a
fiercely Sinn Fein Council while he was
languishing in Belfast Gaol.

More often though there was no humour
whatever, particularly in those parts of the country
where opinion was sharply divided. Differences
arose between groups of staff, so that enginemen
might 'advise' guards not to wave the green flag
(and back up the advice with a gun). People left
jobs rather suddenly, and others were installed or
reinstated equally abruptly. Trains were raided,
sabotage was not unknown, and services were
often suspended. All this may well have been
inevitable given the politics of the time, but was

hardly conducive to good running and railway
discipline. Even then, courage and resolution could
achieve suprising results. Henry Forbes, the
Donegal's Manager, after a gunfight, arrested one
of the armed raiders who had held up a train on
which he was travelling. This may not have excited
the political sympathy of all of his staff, but no
professional railwayman could fail to respect a
boss who was prepared to defend his timetable
with a revolver.

The political settlement which led to the
partition of Ireland did not resolve matters. In the
Free State civil war broke out between
Government and Republican forces. This led to
considerable damage, particularly in County
Cork. Republican forces also occupied the Dingle
peninsula and hijacked a ship off Dingle harbour
in 1922. A special train went flour running to try
and whip up support amongst the hungry
inhabitants of the peninsula. The partition of
Ireland permanently hindered the two main
networks, in that their hinterland in Donegal was
in the Free State, while their centre, Londonderry,
was in Northern Ireland. From then on, all traffic
crossing the border had to pass Customs control.

The return of normal conditions thus found the
railways damaged both by an adverse shift in their
price and cost relationships, and undermined by
several years of physical damage and some
intimidation. Moreover the end of the first world
war saw the advent of road competition in earnest.
In particular this affected the more eastern part of

West Clare train at Kilrush in the early days, with 0–6–0T No 4 (*Leabharlann Naisiunta na hEireann*).

Ireland since the roads in the far west remained appaling. The railways had always been marginal and the change in circumstances made the position desperate. Closures started immediately. The Dublin & Lucan, which had been electrified in the early years of the century, closed in 1924, and in the same year the Listowel & Ballybunion, bankrupt since 1897, shut up shop. The Ballycastle closed in April 1924 but was reopened four months later by the LMS (Northern Counties Committee) anxious about its contributory revenue. The Portstewart Tramway, like the Listowel & Ballybunion, had become insolvent in 1897 but was then bought at auction by the Belfast & Northern Counties, predecessor of the NCC. By 1 January 1926, however, even they had had enough. Closures then came thick and fast. The Cushendall line closed to passengers in 1930 and

to freight between 1937 and 1940. The Cork, Blackrock & Passage closed in 1933 and that same year there was a lengthy strike by railwaymen in Northern Ireland which saw the end of passenger services on the Ballymena & Larne and all services on the Castlederg and Victoria Bridge Tramway. The Lough Swilly decided during the 1920s that its future lay in road rather than rail transport and moved as quickly as it could towards the replacement and closure of its railway system. Only the state of the roads constrained it. The railway was being supported by both Free State and Northern Irish Governments keen to reduce the rail subsidy. However this process could not be pushed too fast; an attempt in 1931 to extend a bus service to Burtenport failed dismally. After eight weeks the buses had to be withdrawn because the roads were

breaking up and the Donegal County Council was demanding substantial compensation. The settlement included an agreement that the Swilly would not run regular bus services into the area without County Council agreement. So the rundown of railway services was controlled but consistent. The first section to lose all railway services was the Carndonagh extension in 1935. In the south, too, more railways were going. The Cork & Muskerry closed in 1935 and the Tralee & Dingle ran its last passenger train in 1939.

Only one railway really fought back. This was the County Donegal under Henry Forbes. In June 1926 the coal strike caused a severe shortage of fuel and as a result a small inspection railcar owned by the County Donegal was used for a number of mail trips. The concept was then rapidly developed. First two standard gauge vehicles were

bought from the Derwent Valley Railway in England and converted to 3ft gauge. By 1931 the Donegal was graduating from petrol to diesel and by opening numbers of new halts and by providing a more frequent and speedy service attracting new custom as well as cutting costs. During the 1930s the cost of steam working fell by about half and the level of railcar working increased five fold. Although the Donegal had a number of years in the early 1930s when it ran at a loss the new form of working proved sufficient to turn this into a reasonable profit by 1939.

The Donegal example was emulated only to a very limited extent. The Clogher Valley was managed from 1929 by a committee with Forbes as one of the members which bought a railcar in 1932 and a small diesel locomotive shortly afterwards. In the south the Great Southern

Railways (which had absorbed all the lines within the Free State in 1925) tried two Drewry railcars between Kilrush and Kilkee on the West Clare from 1928, but otherwise took no action until after the second world war, when the nationalised Coras Iompair Eireann dieselised the West Clare completely in two stages – the passenger service in 1952, and freight in 1955. The only other line to try railcar working was the Castlederg & Victoria Bridge Tramway. That company built its own car in 1925, and thus anticipated the Donegal experiment, but did not have the potential to develop the system.

The second world war affected the various surviving railways very differently. The fuel shortage led to a doubling of traffic on the Donegal, and the Lough Swilly was undoubtedly glad to have retained the skeleton of its railway network. Yet the fuel shortage in the south led to the end of services on the Schull & Skibbereen in April 1944, and the closure of the Clogher Valley at the end of 1941 because of continuing losses which wartime traffic could not reverse.

The period following the end of the war saw further retrenchment. The Schull & Skibbereen reopened at the end of 1945, but closed for good a year later. The Giant's Causeway closed in 1949, and the Ballycastle and remaining freight workings on the Ballymena & Larne stopped the following year. On the Donegal the Glenties line closed in 1947, and the Strabane–Londonderry section in 1954. The L&LSR shut the remaining parts of its lines between 1947 and 1953. The T&D lingered on running a monthly cattle special (presumably cattle lorries were in short supply) until 1953.

This left just three survivors. All met their end in different ways. The Cavan & Leitrim was completely unmodernised and depended for its existence on coal from Arigna. When a power station was built to tap the coal at source the railway was redundant, and closed in 1959. The Donegal ran its remaining lines as efficiently as ever until the end of 1959. Then with neither the funds nor the case for reinvestment it closed. The West Clare went just over a year later as part of a general programme of closing unremunerative railways in the Republic which swept away much broad gauge as well as the last of the narrow gauge.

Today memories and some rolling stock remain. In County Antrim (appropriately) Lord O'Neill has opened a pleasure line in a country park – and some rolling stock has found a home here as well as in the Transport Museum at Belfast. Two locomotives and a few vehicles have also crossed the Atlantic to America. There is another pleasure line at Stradbelly, but these pleasure lines are on a very small scale compared to the old railways. More important to the Irish economy has been the Irish Turf Board's (Bord na Mona) decision to use 3ft gauge lines to serve its turf bogs, carrying the peat to turf-fired power stations in narrow gauge merry-go-round trains. Again, this industrial venture has little relation to the original network.

Perhaps it is best to take stock of the Irish narrow gauge railways when conditions were still similar to those for which they were built. In 1910 they were carrying considerable quantities of traffic. The Swilly carried over half a million passengers and 100,000 tons of goods, making it the busiest line. The Cork, Blackrock & Passage managed over 450,000 passengers and both the Donegal and the Cork & Muskerry over 300,000. Most other lines carried far fewer people. The West Clare had 180,000 but the only other lines with more than 100,000 were the Clogher Valley, the Cavan & Leitrim and the Ballycastle. Freight traffic, too, was rarely up to the levels met on the Lough Swilly. At the other extreme the Schull & Skibbereen was carrying just about 4,500 tons a year.

The Irish narrow gauge railways were subject to considerable criticism and some ridicule. In general this seems to have been based on their financial performance, and assertions that the lines had cost far too much for the traffic available. It is certainly true that there were railways whose financial state varied from the bad to the desperate. The Schull & Skibbereen and Tralee & Dingle in particular had operating ratios which invariably showed working expenses exceeding receipts. However, one should not allow these extreme cases to condition judgement. It was equally true that the Lough Swilly was paying 7 per cent dividends, the highest of any of the Irish railways. It may be that this line was financially successful at some expense to its long term prospects, since there is no doubt that facilities and maintenance were somewhat underdone. However, the Donegal also had a successful profit record and the Castlederg and Victoria Bridge Tramway managed to pay a dividend. By the 1900s the Ballymena lines had been absorbed into the NCC and their individual results lost, but on the basis of their operating ratios it seems likely that they too were profitable. In the same way the charge that

Congested district. On the Lough Swilly at Barnes Gap.
(*Leabharlann Naisiunta na hEireann*).

lines were grossly overbuilt is hard to substantiate. On the contrary there were a number of cases where the original equipment proved decidedly too light. Operating conditions on the Schull & Skibbereen and West Clare lines were chaotic in their early days because of inadequate locomotives. And on the lines built by Government cheeseparing tactics could produce ridiculous results. On the Lough Swilly, station houses had no doorknockers, which saved £2 each. If the lines in Ireland seemed expensive in comparison with some of those in mainland Europe, particularly such countries as Belgium, it was probably because Irish terrain was more difficult (and the climate cannot have made operation easier either).

Was the Irish narrow gauge a successful, worthwhile venture? There is no absolute answer. On financial criteria the result was mixed – as already indicated. The injection of Government money stemmed from broader criteria, of concern about the relative poverty of rural Ireland and about depopulation. The figures show that population continued to fall, and one can only speculate whether the fall would have been greater had the railways not been built. At least the provision of transport facilities was directly linked to the development of suitable industries such as fishing, and success did not depend (as in many more recent cases of road investment) on a blind belief that better transport would itself lead to industrial growth. What is undeniable is that the railways are remembered with affection across the whole spectrum of Irish opinion. It is surely to be regretted that none of the lines has survived to attract tourists to the wild remote places.

Opening ceremonies ranged from the grand to the intimate. The opening of the Crosshaven extension of the Cork, Blackrock & Passage on 30 May, 1904 was definitely in the first category. There were guards of honour, decorated stations and a Reception and Banquet at Haulbowline Naval College. The opening was performed by the Lord Lieutenant himself. The photograph *above* shows the special train at Drakes Pool. The opening of the Schull & Skibbereen, by contrast, on 9 September

1 OPENING

1886 seems to have been mainly marked by a monster sports meeting at Ballydehob. The train, with locomotive No. 3 *Ilen* is shown at Schull, *below*. (*L&GRP; J. F. O'Sullivan Collection*).

Opening of the Crosshaven Extension of the Railway

by his excellency the

Earl of Dudley, K.P.

Lord Lieutenant of Ireland

—◆►◄◆—

⊹§ LUNCHEON ⧽⊱

at

HAULBOWLINE,

By kind permission of Rear-Admiral McLeod, C.V.O.

MAY 30th, 1904.

Top left: A Ballymena & Larne special train leaves Larne Town station and climbs alongside the Larne River during the early days of the railway. The coach is the First Class Saloon — later lent to the Lough Swilly and used for a Royal Train — and the engine appears to be a Beyer Peacock 2—4—0T. Note how many of the houses in Larne were thatched at that time. (*Leabharlann Naisiunta na hEireann*).

Above: 0—6—0T No 108 arrives at Larne Harbour on 3 August 1902. The broad gauge line from Belfast is to the left next to the sea wall, the spur to the narrow gauge turntable to the right. The Harbour station is immediately behind the bridge from which the photograph was taken. (*H. L. Hopwood*).

Left: 2—4—0T No 104 leaving Ballymena for Larne Harbour. The bogie van next to the engine was built in 1892 to handle cross-channel mails. (*L&GRP*).

2 IN COUNTY ANTRIM

Top left: 0—6—0T No 106 approaches Ballymena from the Cushendall line. Both locomotive and coach were Ballymena & Larne stock before both this line and the Ballymena, Cushendall & Red Bay were absorbed by the Belfast & Northern Counties. (*L&GRP*).

Left: The BC&RB had three 0—4—2ST. No 102 shunts at Ballymena between 1897 and 1912. Loaded iron-ore wagons can be seen on the right. (*L&GRP*).

Above: No 102 with a train of coaches specially built by the B&NCR for the tourist traffic to Glenariff. (*L&GRP*).

Top left: The limit of passenger working. No 102 at Parkmore on the BC&RB. (*L&GRP*).

Left: Ballycastle Railway 0–6–0T No 2 waits to leave Ballymoney on 6 May 1920. There is no continuous brake. When the NCC bought the line in 1924 all the Ballycastle stock was scrapped (with the exception of two 4–4–2Ts transferred to the Ballymena & Larne) and replaced by ex B&L stock. (*K. A. C. R. Nunn*).

Above: Ex Ballycastle 4–4–2T No 113 heads a ballast train between Larne Harbour and Larne Town on 22 June 1937. (*S. W. Baker*).

Top left: The Dublin & Lucan ran from Phoenix Park in Dublin to Chapelizoid (1881) and Lucan (1883). An extension to Leixip opened in 1889. As a narrow gauge steam tramway it was short lived. Electric working started between Dublin and Lucan on the 3ft 6in gauge in 1900 – and the Leixip extension was abandoned. The electric line in turn lasted only 24 years – and after four years without any trams at all the line had yet another gauge conversion (to 5ft 3in) and was reopened by the Dublin United Tramways in 1928. In keeping with the best traditions of the line the new service failed to last, buses being substituted in 1940. (*Leabharlann Naisiunta na hEireann*).

Left: The Portstewart Tramway was a modest affair, $1\frac{3}{4}$ miles in length. Its role was to connect the town to the station. Opened in 1882, it was bankrupt by 1897 and bought at auction by the main line company – the Belfast & Northern Counties which later became the Northern Counties Committee of the Midland Railway. The photograph shows tram No 3 at Portstewart early this century. (*Ulster Museum*).

Above: The first section of the Giants Causeway Tramway opened in January 1883. The tramway operated electrically using an elevated third rail which can be seen behind the train in the photograph. It was the world's first lengthy electric tramway. Until 1899 steam locomotives were used through Portrush itself, and at times of heavy traffic. The photograph shows a tram passing Dunluce Castle, ancestral home of the McDonnells, Earls of Antrim. The castle's ruin was nothing to do with the tramway – it dates from 1639 when part of the curtain wall collapsed. (*Leabharlann Naisiunta na hEireann*).

3 ENTER THE TRAMS

Top left: The Cork & Muskerry ran through the streets of Cork City to reach its terminal on Western Road. (Now the Inter Continental Hotel). Early this century a train headed by one of the three original locomotives leaves Cork alongside Cork tram No 18 and a delivery cart. (*W. McGrath Collection*).

Left: 'Stations' could be anything from a stopping place on the road, to elaborate layouts and structures on railway land. Spamont was clearly in the former category, as the 8.15 am from Castlederg to Victoria Bridge paused there on the 21 May, 1924. The locomotive was C&VBT 0–4–4T No 5. (*K. A. C. R. Nunn*).

Above: Most animals became accustomed to steam horses alongside them. This horse on the Schull & Skibbereen looks more inclined to race! The photograph is also of interest in showing 0–4–4T 6S, formerly Cork & Muskerry No 6 *The Muskerry*. (*W. Briggs, W. McGrath Collection*).

4 BY THE ROADSIDE

A New Song of the Clogher Valley Line
Anon. 1887. Try tune of the Enniskillen Dragoons

In the second of May we must say in this present year,
We opened up the new tramway from what we read and hear,
This lovely rail from hill and dale it cut a lovely shine,
From Tynon to Maguire's Bridge on the Clogher Valley Line.

It sends the farmers of Fermanagh and all South Tyrone,
To Omagh now or Fintona they have no cause to roam,
From Fivemiletown to Aughnacloy on every market day,
They can bring their pork also their flax all by the new tramway.

The old wife in the corner has no cause to complain,
She can bring her butter and her eggs all by the morning train,
Unto her house and family she can return in time,
For a half fare we must declare on the Clogher Valley Line.

Through Fermanagh and Tyrone this tramway it does run,
We read and find along the line all things are nicely done,
We can lift passengers on the road, and also in the town,
By this tramway from day to day that runs both up and down.

The distinction between a rural tramway and a light railway was nowhere more tenuous than in Ireland. Several lines changed their title from tramway to light railway, and both could equally well run on or alongside a road. The Clogher Valley ran alongside the road for much of its length — and right up the main street of Fivemiletown. As the song commemorating the opening has it *this is the whole vexation*. The situation seems much the same here — in the year before closure. (*J. K. Clarke*).

From Maguire's Bridge the tram does start I wish to explain,
There is a grand view as she runs through part of Colebrook Demesne,
You get a sight of Blessingburn and the See of Clogher too,
Round Ballygawley and Carrongal there is a splendid view.

We cannot forget our Irish members that passed this tramway Bill,
Mr Montgomery sanctioned it we are sure with free good will,
With Mr Graham a man of fame and others did combine,
To open up our country with the Clogher Valley Line.

Our engines and our carriages they look both grand and neat,
With the buildings all along the line they are finished off complete,
This is the key to Ulster you must all bear in mind,
From Fivemiletown to Caledon on the Clogher Valley Line.

This new tramway three times a day she runs both up and down,
The most mistakes I'm sure they make it is at Fivemiletown,
She clears the streets of all she meets it is the whole vexation,
Going up and down through the town to and from the station.

5 ODD MAN OUT

Left: The Listowel & Ballybunion was quite the most peculiar of the Irish railways. It was built by the Lartigue Railway Construction Company to demonstrate M. Lartigue's system of monorails. As the single rail was raised some 3ft 6in above the ground everything was divided or duplicated. The railway was in a remote part of County Kerry and traffic was low. It went into receivership in 1897. This early view shows 0–3–0 No 1, one of the three locomotives, at Ballybunion. It is just clear of the turntable, which took the place of the points on a more conventional line. The photograph illustrates the 'divided' construction necessary with the system. Loads had to be balanced on each side of the rail, and if the tales told of the line are to be believed a passenger was as likely to share his half coach with a calf as with a fellow human. (*Leabharlann Naisiunta na hEireann*).

Bottom left: Leaving Listowel. Intriguingly, the left hand engine seems to be working harder than its opposite number. Was this necessary on all right hand curves? The monorail did not save any space. The sleepers appear long enough to have supported 3ft gauge tracks, and the total weight of ironwork supporting the monorail far exceeded that required for the two ground level rails on a conventional system. So what was the advantage of the Lartigue monorail? (*Leabharlann Naisiunta na hEireann*).

Below: The railway was 'hinged' for occupation (farm) crossings. Public roads demanded something more elaborate – such as this drawbridge. When the drawbridge was lowered, the signal in the middle of the span was raised to warn approaching trains. (*L&GRP*).

6 GUARANTEED BY THE BARONIES

Six complete railways were built under district council guarantee — the Irish districts at the time being known as Baronies. This led to railways being built where local people wanted them, but often where the commercial prospects were indifferent. Most of the lines ran alongside the road for part of the way, but the nature of the country made heavy engineering works inevitable. The twelve arch viaduct, *left*, across Roaringwater bay at Ballydehob on the Schull & Skibbereen is one of the most impressive survivors. The locomotive appears to be *Gabriel*, and the date soon after 1906. (*Leabharlann Naisiunta na hEireann*).

Below right: Ballydehob in 1939 looking across the viaduct. Because the site on the opposite side of the water does not look any more difficult it seems strange that the station was on one side of Roaringwater Bay — and the town on the other. The locomotive is 4–4–0T No 4. (*J. K. Clarke*).

Below left: Schull station, like most on the narrow gauge, was (and is) a substantial building. (*Leabharlann Naisiunta na hEireann*).

Above: 4–4–0T No 4 after being turned on Schull turntable — the engine shed is to the right with an elegant early nineteenth century house behind. (*Lens of Sutton*).

Below: The Cork & Muskerry opened its first section in 1887 — along with the West Clare, the Clogher Valley (illustrated elsewhere in the book) and the Cavan & Leitrim. Sunday excursions to Blarney — such as this one shown on Carrigrohane around the turn of the century — were a regular attraction for sportsmen and family parties. (*L&GRP*).

Right: The Muskerry Foxhounds meet at Leemont station early this century. The railway left the road and went onto its own right of way just behind the house. Anyone who has read Somerville and Ross' famous tales will know the association between railways and hunting in County Cork. (*W. McGrath Collection*).

Above: Ballinamore was the hub of the Cavan & Leitrim. The Arigna branch bay is to the left and the works to the right. The locomotive is in original condition and the date 1903. (*H. Fayle Courtesy IRRS*).

Top right: No 8 at Dromod with the 12.45 from Belturbet on 17 May, 1924. Originally *Queen Victoria* the nameplates were removed by enginemen with strong republican leanings during the troubles! (*K. A. C. R. Nunn*).

Right: The Cavan & Leitrim accumulated a number of engines from other lines as these closed. The first were the four CB&P 2—4—2Ts which arrived in 1933. 13L (formerly CB&P No 7) is at Dromod in 1937. (*J. M. Jarvis*).

The twin West Clare terminals. Kilkee and Kilrush shortly after the line was completely opened in 1892. In the early days the service was less reliable than these elegant photographs *above* and *below* might suggest — leading to Percy French's famous satirical song *Are Ye Right There Michael*? (*Leabharlann Naisiunta na hEireann*).

Are Ye Right There Michael?

They may talk of Columbus' sailing,
Across the Atlantical sea,
But sure he never went railing,
From Ennis as far as Kilkee.
You run for the train in the morning,
The excursion train starting at eight,
You're there when the clock gives the warning,
And there for an hour you'll wait.
And as you're sitting in the train,
You'll hear the guard sing this refrain;
'Are ye right there Michael, are ye right?
'Do ye think that we'll be there before the night?
'Ye couldn't say for sartain, ye were so late in startin',
'But we might now Michael, so we might.'

They find out where the engine's been hiding,
And it draws you to sweet Corofin,
Says the guard, 'Back her down in the siding,
There's the goods from Kilrush comin' in.'
Perhaps it comes in two hours,
Perhaps it breaks down on the way,
'If it does,' says the guard, 'By the powers,
'We're here for the rest of the day.'
And as you sit and curse your luck,
The train backs down on to a truck,
'Are ye right there Michael, are ye right?
'Have ye got the parcel there for Mrs White?
'Ye haven't, Oh begorra, say it's coming down to-morrow,
'And it might now, Michael, so it might.'

At Lahinch the sea shines like a jewel,
With joy you are ready to shout,
When the stoker cries out 'We've no fuel,
'And the fire's taytotally out,
'But give us a hand with that log there,
'I'll soon get ye out of a fix,
'There's a fine clamp of turf in the bog there,
'And the rest go a-gathering sticks.'
And while you're breaking bits off trees,
You'll hear some wise remarks like these:
'Are ye right there Michael, are ye right?
'Do you think that ye can get the fire to light?
'Oh an hour you'll require, for the turf it might be drier,
'And it might now Michael, so it might.'

Kilkee, Oh you never get near it,
You're in luck if the train brings you back,
For the permanent way is so queer, it
Spends most of its time off the track.
Uphill the old engine is toiling,
The passengers push with a will,
You're in luck when you reach Ennistymon,
For all the way home is downhill,
And as you're wobbling through the dark,
You'll hear the guard make this remark:
'Are ye right there Michael, are ye right?
'Do ye think that we'll be home before the light?
''Tis all dependin' whether the old engine holds together,
'But we might now Michael so we might.'

Percy French, courtesy McCullough Pigott Ltd, Dublin

The South Clare Railway extended the West Clare from Miltown Malbay to Kilrush and Kilkee and opened in August 1892. The engineer building the line was persuaded to run a pig special before the line was complete and this came to grief somewhere near Moyasta. The locomotive is 0–6–0T No 2. (*W. McGrath Collection*).

The goods shed at Ennis was still under construction when 0–6–2T No 7 *Lady Inchiquin* was photographed there in September 1898. (*H. L. Hopwood*).

Of all the railways the Tralee & Dingle had the most sustained and ferocious gradients. Annascaul came between the two summits at Glenagalt and Garrynadur and was the second crossing point. The railway towards Tralee climbed alongside the road in the left background, at 1 in 29. (*Leabharlann Naisiunta na hEireann*).

Casual working over the T&D's gradients and curves led to the Curraduff disaster on 22 May 1893. A pig special from Dingle got out of control and derailed on the approach to the viaduct over the River Finglas, just below Camp village. The three men on the footplate (and about 90 pigs) were killed, and 13 passengers injured. The *Irish Times* reporter obviously did not see the pathos of his comments. (*W. MacCarthy*).

UNINJURED PIGS REACH CORK

A consignment of six uninjured pigs, survivors of the dread crash at Camp on Monday, was today received in the Cork Bacon Factory of Messrs. Lunhams. A spokesman said they had all escaped injury.

(*Irish Times* 26 May, 1893)

Hunslet 2–6–0T No 6 ready to leave Tralee on the 8.30 to
Dingle in July 1914. (*K. A. C. R. Nunn*).

Final year of independence. 2–6–2T No 5 at the new
station at Dingle in 1924. (*K. A. C. R. Nunn*).

Loads could be heavy. This pig special at Auchnacloy on
the Clogher Valley in 1937 required to be double headed
by 0–4–2Ts No 6 and No 3. (*L&GRP*).

7 LIVESTOCK

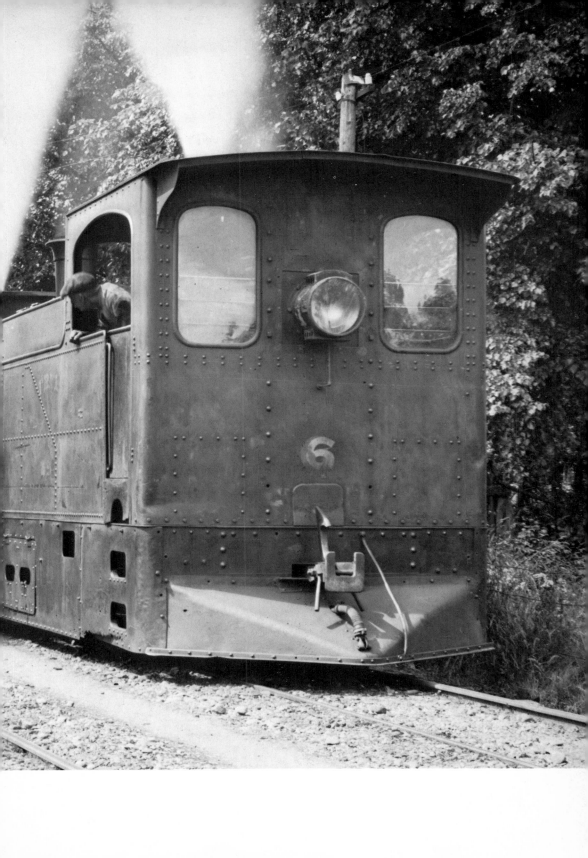

In a pastoral country livestock markets provided a most important source of traffic. The fairs were not only major business occasions, but also great social gatherings in small towns. Cattle had to be driven to the station for loading. 2–6–0T No 1 shunts the cattle dock at Dingle in 1907. (*H. Fayle, courtesy IRRS*).

8 EXCURSIONISTS

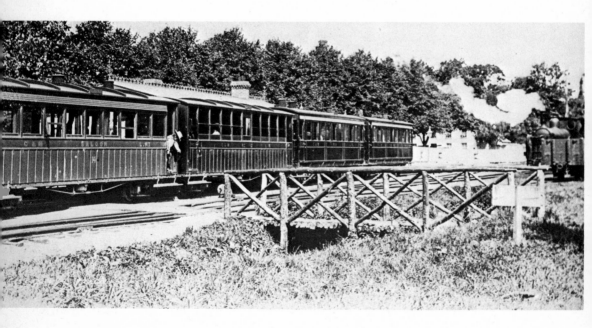

At the turn of the century many of the lines were fitted out to cater for excursionists. Nowhere was this more evident than on the Cork & Muskerry where weekend traffic to Blarney was heavy. In the photograph *below left* the C&MLR's first No 4 *Blarney* – an 0–4–2WT – runs round its train, while *above* 4–4–0T *Peake* waits to depart for Cork. (*J. Wills, collection J. Harrison; L&GRP*).

Below: The West Clare, despite its relatively remote position, built a special series of saloons for tourist traffic, complete with large observation windows and the most marvellous Victorian stained glass. Coach 34 and van No 2 are headed by one of the three 0–6–2Ts built by Dübs in 1892. (*V. Goldberg Collection*).

9 GOVERNMENT RAILWAYS

Left: After neither private enterprise nor local authority guarantees proved sufficient to drive railways into the more remote districts, the Government built them itself and arranged for existing companies to work them. The first such line was the extension from Donegal to Killybegs. Six 4–6–0Ts were delivered to the Donegal to help work the line, and one of these No 5 *Drumboe* waits to leave Killybegs in 1902. (*H. Fayle Courtesy IRRS*).

Overleaf: The second extension took the Donegal metals across the River Finn from Stranorlar. One of the Donegal's first locomotives, 2–4–0T No 3 *Lydia* of 1883, pauses on the new bridge with Stranorlar church and station behind. (*Ulster Museum*).

10 LOUGH SWILLY

Top left: The Lough Swilly over the 12 miles from Londonderry to Buncrana was originally built as a broad gauge line, and converted to 3ft gauge in the mid 1880s. This early photograph of Buncrana shows 0–6–2T No 1 *J. T. Macky*. (*L&GRP*).

Left: Steamers carried both freight and passengers on Lough Swilly in conjunction with the railway services to Fahan Pier, south of Buncrana. PS *Lake of Shadows* is beached behind the new 1922 pier at Fahan in this view, and the station building is visible just behind the crane. (*L&GRP*).

Above: 4–8–4T No 6 on a Sunday excursion at Buncrana in 1931. The Swilly had a large excursion traffic which survived until 1951. The train is standing at the new platform, connected to the original platform shown in the earlier photographs by the footbridge. (*L&GRP*).

We go to Fahan to have a 'dip'
And stroll along the strand,
Then up the road to have a cup
Of coffee at the Stand.
The Barmaid she is charming
With her you can remain
Until it's time for to go back
On the 'Buncrana Train'.

Anon 1890s

Above: The Swilly obtained two Government-built extensions as a result of the 1896 Act. The first 18 miles from Buncrana to Carndonagh opened in 1901. One of the 4–6–2Ts is being watered using what looks like a garden hose. The company squabbled continually with Government about the latter's cheeseparing, while the Government in turn was never satisfied that the company maintained its assets properly. (*Leabharlann Naisiunta na hEireann*).

Top right: The second extension was no less than 49 miles long, from Letterkenny to Burtonport, a bleak fishing port on the Atlantic coast. 4–6–2T No 13 was the engine on the train for Letterkenny and Londonderry in 1931, while the rocky nature of terrain at Burtonport is evident. (*L&GRP*).

Right: The Swilly had a curiously inadequate terminal at Londonderry Graving Dock. No 8, another 4–6–2T, shunts in May 1937. (*R. G. Jarvis*).

The viaduct at Owencarrow was the scene of one of the worst accidents on the Irish narrow gauge in January 1925, when a train was derailed in a gale. The event is commemorated by D. Hay in the manner of McGonegal. The weather was rather kinder when this early view was taken. (*Leabharlann Naisiunta na hEireann*).

The Viaduct Disaster

On a wild and stormy winter's night,
The little train did steam,
Adown past Kilmacrenan,
And Lurgy's purling stream,
She passed along down through the Gap,
The Owencarrow she passed by,
Until she reached the hills of Doe,
Beneath an angry sky.

A sudden gust came from above;
Two carriages were swept o'er,
Three passengers there met their death,
Leaving hearts both sad and sore.
One other soul did pass away,
Her race on earth is done,
She died in Letterkenny,
At the rising of the dawn.

A band of noble heroes,
Came from far and near;
They worked to save the wounded,
With neither dread nor fear.
Bold lads from Kilmacrenan,
And from the vales of Doe,
Worked hard and sore together,
In that valley full of woe.

Near the village of Falcarragh,
There are hearts both sad and sore,
God help that distressed family,
On the Isle of Arranmore.
I hope and trust the wounded
Will soon be strong again —
That they will all recover
From all their grief and pain.

God help that little family
Living up beside the Gap,
They lost their loving father
In that unfortunate mishap.
I can't mention individuals,
But must give praise to one and all,
Who helped in the disaster
'Mid the hills of Donegal.

The officials of the Railway,
Worked hard with craft and skill;
Each one did play a noble part
Their duties to fulfil —
To assist the sufferers in distress,
In their lonely, weary plight.
Long will our memories wander back,
To that stormy winter's night.

D. Hay, undated.

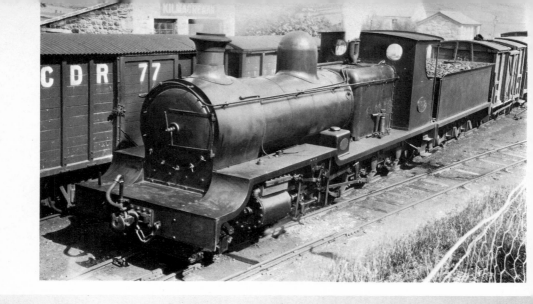

Left: 4–8–0 No 12 at Kilmacrenan in 1931. The large 4–8–0s were well suited to the 74-mile run from Londonderry to Burtonport. (*L&GRP*).

11 CORK, BLACKROCK & PASSAGE

Below: The Cork, Blackrock & Passage was the last of the three lines which converted from 5ft 3in to 3ft gauge. Like the Lough Swilly it also ran extensive steamer services. The narrow gauge did not in this instance lead to low costs or to any relaxation of standards as is pretty evident from this early photograph of Crosshaven. (*Leabharlann Naisiunta na hEireann*).

Above: Inside Ballinamore Works on the C&L. (*H. Fayle Courtesy IRRS*).

Top right: The 15 4–6–0Ts worked on the Donegal (6), Lough Swilly (4) and West Clare (5) lines. The first two classes were built to work Government railways built under the 1889 and 1896 Acts, and were generally similar. Excellent engines within their limitations, they were nonetheless rather underprovided with coal and water when the length of haul out to Burtonport is considered. Letterkenny & Burtonport Extension Railway No 2 poses on the turntable at Burtonport in July 1935. (*J. M. Jarvis*).

Bottom right: The West Clare 4–6–0Ts were slightly larger at 36–40 tons. They were generally similar though the last two (1922), the last new steam locomotives built for the Irish narrow gauge, had outside valve gear. WCR No 11 *Kilkee* was built in 1909 and photographed at Ennis in August 1935. (*J. M. Jarvis*).

Overleaf, left

Top: The Belfast & Northern Counties (and its successor the Northern Counties Committee) developed a class of six compound 2–4–2Ts which were used on the Ballymena & Larne, Ballymena, Cushendall & Red Bay and (after 1924) on the Ballycastle. NCC No 111 was one of the first engines of the class, built in 1892; the last followed 28 years later. (*R. G. Jarvis*).

Centre: The largest locomotives were (not surprisingly) found on the two longest systems, the County Donegal and the Lough Swilly. The policies of the two railways differed. The Donegal had good track and accepted axle loads up to $10\frac{1}{2}$ tons. Its large engines were six-coupled tanks, of which the first, four 4–6–4Ts, appeared in 1904. *Erne* was photographed at Glenties in 1935. (*J. M. Jarvis*).

Bottom: The Lough Swilly on the other hand put a high priority on low axleloads. The two 4–8–0s (illustrated elsewhere) had the very low axle weight of $6\frac{1}{2}$ tons, and it seems surprising in retrospect that the Swilly did not stick with this successful design. However when two further locomotives were required in 1910 the company experimented with a large 4–6–2T design, and in 1912 obtained two remarkable 4–8–4Ts, initially part of the Letterkenny & Burtonport Extension stock. These were the largest engines on the narrow gauge and weighed as much as the 4–8–0s and their tenders ($58\frac{3}{4}$ tons). (*J. M. Jarvis*).

Overleaf, right

13 ROLLING STOCK

Top: Narrow gauge rolling stock was of great variety, some with side doors, others with end-balcony entrances. They could be four, six or eight-wheeled. The Schull & Skibbereen had a mixture of four wheeled and bogie stock, two of the former being shown here in 1935. (*H. Fayle Courtesy IRRS*).

Centre: The finest vehicles were the corridor coaches turned out by the NCC in 1928. Four were completely new and one a rebuild on an old Ballymena & Larne frame. The bodysides were built up from standard parts used at Derby to construct LMS coaches. The main use for these excellent coaches was on the boat trains from Larne to Ballymena, connecting there with Belfast to Londonderry trains. Later some of the coaches were used on the Ballycastle, and the Donegal. This one is a brake third rebuilt as a third. (*L&GRP*).

Bottom: Donegal Third Saloon No 29 was built in 1905, an elegant example of its period. (*H. Fayle Courtesy IRRS*).

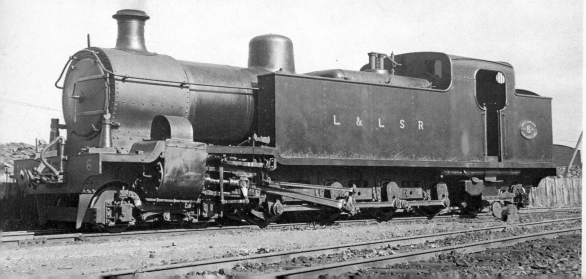

The four-wheeled wagon was the most common, and most important, vehicle. This Cavan & Leitrim vehicle is a relatively sophisticated example. It is a convertible ventilated wagon capable of carrying either merchandise or cattle. (*H. Fayle Courtesy IRRS*).

Disputes and disorders marked the period leading up to the partition of Ireland — and for the next two years civil war raged in the south between Government (Free State) and republican forces. All the railways suffered 'incidents' in one or both conflicts — some lines were closed for various periods and others were sabotaged. One of the latter was the Cork, Blackrock & Passage. Free State forces landed at Passage to march on Cork which was in republican hands. Rochestown Bridge was between and was blown up by the republicans. The photographs (*below left, above and below*) show it being repaired by railway troops of the Irish Army. (*W. McGrath collection*).

14 THE TROUBLES

The end of the first world war left the railways with greatly inflated costs, and serious competition from road for the first time. To this unpromising mixture the troubles added their own measure of damage and undermined authority. Yet while several railways had to pack up shop others fought back with determination. The basis for the struggle was to be the small petrol-engined inspection cars which several companies had bought. The Tralee & Dingle car dated from 1922. It was 10ft 6in long and 6ft wide. It was later based on the West Clare where it was photographed shortly before closure — still used for its original purpose. (W. McGrath).

15 INTER-WAR ENTERPRISE

The Donegal had a rather similar vehicle which dated from 1907, and had been rebuilt in 1920. In the 1926 coal strike it took the place of a steam mail train on the Glenties branch, and its success in this limited role led to the steady construction of larger railcars. In this photograph taken at Stranorlar in 1932 the pioneer railcar No 1 is shown coupled to lightweight trailer No 5 of 1929. This trailer, which dwarfs the railcar, would itself seem tiny next to a conventional coach. (L&GRP).

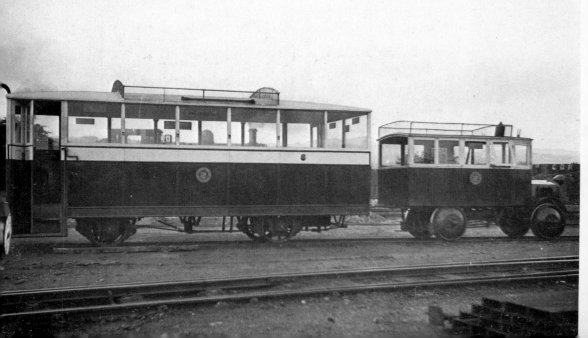

A major step forward was taken in 1931 when the first two Donegal diesel railcars arrived. They had a front radial truck, and drive was to a rear bogie. No 8 waits at the main platform at Stranorlar. (*Lens of Sutton*).

The railcars handled the basic passenger service and were quite capable of towing several trailers for passengers parcels or general goods. This photograph is at Stranorlar with the points set for the Glenties branch. The date is 23 June, 1937, and the railcar seems to be either 15 or 16. (*S. W. Baker*).

Above: Railcar triumphant! The turntable at Killybegs was built from the main frame of one of the 4–6–0T locomotives. Railcar 16 is shown in 1957. The locomotive shed at Killybegs was demolished when a steam train left on the wrong road – ran into the shed and pushed the end wall into the harbour. This brought the roof down on to the engine, and knocked the chimney off. However the crew managed to extricate the engine and set off for Donegal. Needless to say, the train did not get far and a relief engine was sent for. Somehow the men succeeded in 'not troubling' the manager with this particular incident. (*F. W. Shuttleworth*).

Top left: Donegal, with railcar No 16 and trailer No 2. The trailer was built on the chassis of the car which had kept services going on the Castlederg & Victoria Bridge Tramway between 1925 and 1928. (*Lens of Sutton*).

Left: The advent of the railcars reduced the need for steam locomotives, and by 1937 the Donegal had withdrawn all its steam fleet except the 4–6–4Ts and 2–6–4Ts. These were superheated and worked the goods and excursion traffic, plus the line between Londonderry and Strabane which remained a steam preserve. In the photograph, *left*, one of the 2–6–4Ts stands on an excursion train at Strabane platform, while on the back cover 4–6–4T No 10 *Owenea* leaves Strabane for Stranorlar in May 1937. (*Lens of Sutton; back cover photograph, R. G. Jarvis*).

Most of the steam work was related to goods working. Here 2–6–4T No 6 *Columbkille* shunts at Letterkenny in 1957. (*F. W. Shuttleworth*).

By the early 1930s the Donegal was energetically building up its railcar fleet, using both new and secondhand equipment. With its own workshops at Stranorlar, a local coachbuilder at Strabane, and the Great Northern's works at Dundalk, the railway was equipped to tackle most opportunities. In 1934 the railway bought its first bogie railcar, No 12. It is seen here on test. Vacuum brake and couplers were soon fitted. (*Lens of Sutton*).

Another of Forbes' bargains was *Phoenix*. This was an unsuccessful steam tractor on the Clogher Valley. Forbes bought it for 100 guineas in 1932 and Dundalk rebuilt it with a Gardiner Diesel engine. From then on it spent much of the time shunting the exchange sidings at Strabane, and working wagons out to the customs posts at Castlefinn and Lifford. (*F. W. Shuttleworth*).

The Great Southern, which had absorbed those lines which were entirely within the Free State in 1925, tried out railcars in a modest way in 1928. Two Drewry cars were purchased and used between Kilrush and Kilkee. The photograph was taken in 1933 and shows car No 396. The railcars remained peripheral to the West Clare operation, however, and were scrapped in 1943. (*L&GRP*).

The reaction to change on the NCC lines in the north east of Ireland was more conventional. It was felt that steam traction was satisfactory, but that the comfort of ageing narrow gauge coaches left a lot to be desired. New corridor stock was built, *left*, primarily for use on the boat trains which carried passengers from Larne Harbour to connect with trains to Londonderry at Ballymena. Excellent though this stock was, it did not long prolong the life of the railway. All passenger services ceased in 1933. The new coaches were then transferred to the Ballycastle, where two of them are shown, *above*, at Ballymoney behind 2–4–2T No 101; later three were bought by the Donegal. (*LPC; L&GRP*).

The Clogher Valley was one of the few railways to take note of the Donegal's example. It had been taken over by a Committee of Management of Tyrone and Fermanagh County Councils in 1928, and Henry Forbes was made a member of the Committee. In 1932 the CVR obtained the first bogie railcar to work on the Irish narrow gauge — the prototype of several on the Donegal and West Clare. This photograph shows the railcar at Fivemiletown in 1937. (*R. G. Jarvis*).

16 COMMITTEE OF MANAGEMENT

CVR diesel unit at Fivemiletown in May 1937. This was similar to the front bogie and cab of the railcar but attached to a truck body. In essence it acted as a railcar — or, as the current timetables had it, a rail coach — towing a van and a coach. It probably did not ride well and offered little compensating advantage over railcars; certainly all further production was in railcar form. (*R. G. Jarvis*).

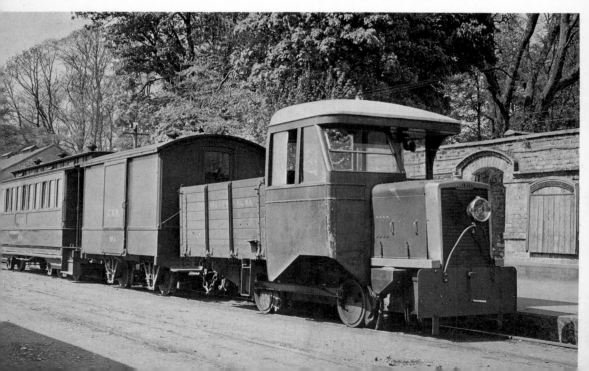

The train pauses at Clogher on its way to Maguiresbridge in 1933. On ordinary days there was one steam working to supplement the rail coaches. This had to handle much of the freight. The station buildings on the CVR (in common with most of the lines) were to a high standard. Note the fanlight above the door into the water tower. (*L&GRP*).

Anon poem about Tommy Caruth, CVR guard, 1940

Tommy the Guard

It's Clogher Fair
and we're running late
And Tommy the guard's
in a terrible state
For its bad enough
he's heard to say
To miss the Mail
on an ordin'ry day.

For people, says he
if they're left behind
Can look after themselves
without they're blind
But bastes, says he
as he peers ahead
If they're left behind
has got to be fed
And the Manager'll curse
to bate the ban
At fattening bastes
for a dealing man.

The carriages dance
in the August heat
And Tommy sits down
in the corner seat
His ticket punch
slides to the floor
And Tommy the guard
begins to snore
For its hard enough
at the best of times
To manage a train
at seventy nine.

CLOGHER VALLEY RAILWAY
Diesel Rail Coach Service

SUMMER
TIME TABLE

**FIRST-CLASS TRAVEL AT
THIRD-CLASS FARE : :**

For further particulars apply to—
D. N. McCLURE,
GENERAL MANAGER,
AUGHNACLOY.

Above: Crickly Halt, between Tynan and Aughnacloy. The line ran alongside the road for much of its route, which made it very susceptible to competition, and the deficits were heavy. Nevertheless the introduction of diesel working made a substantial impression, roughly doubling passenger journeys to about 50,000 a year. (*L&GRP*).

Below: The Committee did all they could to economise. One example of mechanisation was the weed killing train. Note nozzles to spray both the ballast and the trackside. (*L&GRP*).

Left: CVR timetable June 1939.

The CVR's 0—4—4T No 7 *Blessingbourne* was prone to slipping and hardly satisfactory. In 1935 she was exchanged (plus the remains of 0—4—2T No 1) for CVBT 2—6—0T No 4, which had been bought by a Belfast contractor. This locomotive was rebuilt at Aughnacloy into a 2—6—2T, providing a powerful supplement to the steam fleet — by then down to three of the original 0—4—2Ts. The photographs of this locomotive exchange show No 7 *above* and No 4 *below* at Aughnacloy in 1933 and 1937 respectively. (*L&GRP; R. G. Jarvis*).

Right: The roadside lines hit (or were hit by) just about everything probable — and most things improbable. The Dingle was in collison with a circus in 1940. However without doubt the most bizarre accident occurred *right* when a steam roller ran into the 7.45 am from Donoughmore to Cork in 1927. The tale is told in the extract from the diary of a passenger. This occurred only a few years before the line closed, inspiring the 'Lament for the Blarney Express' (Hook and eye was a nickname for the line presumably derived from the couplings). (*W McGrath collection*).

7 MINOR INCIDENT

SEPTEMBER, 1927.

Tuesday 6
(249-116)

A fine day after a wet night. To Cork. A collision occurred at Inchigaggin between tram & steam roller, through default of latter. One carriage badly damaged and turned partly on its side. Another and engine (tram) slightly damaged and steam roller broken in front. Driver of latter slightly injured. Passengers escaped injury but a basket of eggs belonging to a Donoughmore man were broken. I walked into town with a Bloghroe girl and helped to carry her basket of eggs. Dermot came later carrying ducks & books. Came home by 6 rain which was late. At boot auction Bt 1 pr ladies br shoes 9/6 1 pr boys 1 Els 6/4 1 pr white buck Els 11 or 12 4/3 — 1 pr ladies br shoes Flat (Brn) 10/6 1 pr boys Els 8/- 1 pr El Els (10) 10/- Julia Dowling won £30 Scholarship for 5 years. Got coupon for "Daily Mail Insurance re Conditions on Daily Mail of 13 April 1927 (No 9,788)

Lament for the Blarney Express

Goodbye, goodbye
Old Hook an' Eye
Farewell, O Harnessed Power!
We knew full well
The strain would tell
At fourteen miles an hour!

Sometimes you'd touch
Fifteen — too much
You couldn't well outlast them
When there were snails,
Between your rails
You very often passed 'em.

They're sick and sore
At Donoughmore
They weep at Coachford Junction
Away out West
By the Angler's Rest
Their fishing rods won't function.

While at St. Anne's
The porter scans
The up-line, fairly hoping
Men sit and groan
With hearts of stone
At Blarney, grimly moping.

Your own old bell
Has tolled your knell;
You've lost your head of pressure
One final blow —
Then off you go —
Good-bye, old friend — and bless you.

18 LAST DAYS ON THE TRALEE & DINGLE

Below: The road to Dingle was metalled in 1939, and this led to the complete closure of the branch and the reduction of the main line to freight only status. The passenger stock sat idle in Tralee Station yard when Kenneth Clarke visited the railway in the summer of 1939. (*J. K. Clarke*).

Right: After 1947 the service was restricted to monthly cattle specials in conjunction with Dingle Fair. The railway was very run down and legends have grown up around the events which occurred in working these trains over fearsome gradients on an almost unmaintained railway. 2–6–0T No 1T is seen on a loaded cattle train on Lispole Viaduct in 1953. Double heading over the viaduct was forbidden due to corrosion of the centre spans. This was one occasion when the rule was observed. No 8T was backing down to recouple when the photograph was taken. (*D. G. Rowlands Collection*).

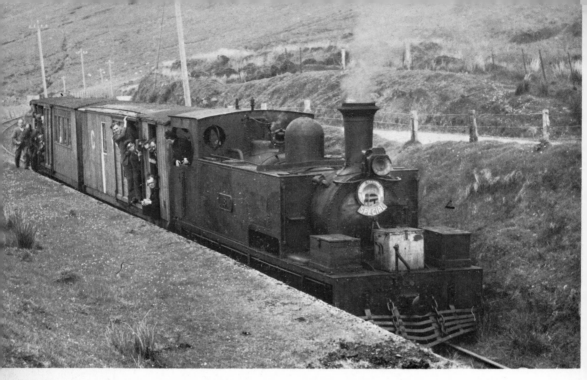

Above: The last passenger train was a special organised by the Light Railway Transport League in June 1953, photographed here at Glengalt Bridge platform. (*Lens of Sutton*)

Below: A double-headed empty cattle special climbs the bank out of Annuscaul in June 1952. The Connemara pony in the foreground appears quite unconcerned at the invasion of his grazing. (*R. N. Clements*).

19 TO THE END

The last three lines went within two years, the Cavan & Leitrim on 31 March, 1959, the Donegal on 31 December that same year, and the West Clare on 31 January 1961. The end came for different reasons. The Cavan & Leitrim had survived to carry coal from one of Ireland's very few pits, at Arigna. A power station was eventually built on Lough Allen to absorb the whole coal output and that was that. The fuel went out over the wires and not in narrow gauge wagons. In the photograph *top right* ex Tralee & Dingle 2–6–0T No 3T leaves Arigna with empty wagons for the colliery, while *below right* the same engine takes water before leaving for Ballinamore with a loaded train in August 1956. (*Lens of Sutton; N. F. Gurley*).

Top left: The tramway between Ballinamore and Arigna followed the road, and had plenty of short gradients. 3T rushes one between Creagh and Kilubrid with the 4.15 from Arigna on 16 March 1957. (*B. Hilton*).

Left: The railway may have been scruffy and worn out, but there was plenty of activity at Ballinamore right to the end. 3T waits to leave for Arigna on 14 March 1959, while one of the railway's original 4—4—0Ts blows off on shed. (*B. Hilton*).

Above: Two days later 6T arrives from Dromod on the 12.20 to Belturbet, with the Arigna train shunting beyond the crossing. (*B. Hilton*).

Top left: The donkey was eventually persuaded to back up to the van, and allow the parcels to be transferred. Creagh, 16 March, 1959. (*B. Hilton*).

Left: No 6T leaves Ballinamore on the 8.0 am to Dromod on 16 March 1959. (*B. Hilton*).

The Donegal provided an excellent service to the end; it only closed when major renewals became due and there were no funds for them. The form of working remained that established in the 1930s and could be complex. The three photographs on this and following pages were taken at Castlefin in 1956. Railcar No 14, bound for Stranolar has run wrong line past the eastbound mixed train, *above*, and backed down behind it, *next page*. This then allowed railcar 12 for Strabane to overtake the mixed, *page 90*. (*N. F. Gurley*).

(EXCEPT WHERE OTHERWISE STATED TH[...]

	a.m.	a.m.	a.m.		a.m.	p.m.	p.m.	p.m.	**A** p.m.	noo[...]
Letterkenny dep.	...	...	8 45	...	10 50	2 35	6 0	...	7 25	...
Convoy ... ,,	...	...	9 12	...	11 22	3 11	6 22	...	7 50	...
Raphoe ... ,,	...	...	9 18	...	11 33	3 22	6 34	...	8 1	...
Lifford ... arr.	...	...	9 37	...	11 53	3 43	6 54	...	8 20	...
Lifford ... dep.	...	...	9 44	...	11 58	3 49	6 56	...	8 26	...
Strabane ... arr.	...	...	9 45	...	12 0	3 50	6 58	...	8 28	...

						B			**A**	
Strabane ... dep.	7 20	9 10	11 10	...	2 20	4 10	...	6 15	7 30	...
Castlefin ... arr.	7 42	9 35	11 30	...	2 40	4 29	...	6 34	7 47	
Castlefin ... dep.	7 43	9 36	11 35	...	2 45	4 30	...	6 37	7 50	
Killygordon ... ,,	7 54	9 45	11 48	...	2 58	4 39	...	6 47	8 0	
Stranorlar ... arr.	8 5	9 56	12 2	...	3 11	4 50	...	6 55	8 10	
									A	
Stranorlar ... dep.	8 6	...	12 5	...	3 15	4 51	...	7 0	...	
Donegal ... arr.	9 0	...	1 5	...	4 15	5 47	...	7 58	...	

					A	**B**		**A**		**C**
Donegal ... dep.	9 10	...	1 25	...	5 55	6 10	...	8 5	...	...
Ballintra ... ,,	9 36	...	1 51	...	6 21	6 36	...	8 31	...	...
Rossnowlagh ... ,,	9 49	...	2 4	...	6 34	6 49	...	8 44	...	12 [...]
Ballyshannon ... arr.	10 10	...	2 25	...	6 55	7 10	...	9 5	...	12 2[...]

								A		
Donegal ... dep.	9 5	...	1 10	...	4 20	...	...	8 0	...	
Mountcharles ... ,,	9 20	...	1 27	...	4 36	...	...	8 16	...	
Inver ... ,,	9 34	...	1 41	...	4 49	...	...	8 29	...	
Dunkineely ... ,,	9 49	...	1 57	...	5 4	...	...	8 43	...	
Killybegs ... arr.	10 15	...	2 22	...	5 29	...	...	9 8	...	

A—Saturdays only.
B—Saturdays excepted.
C—Sundays only.

Time Table

(SERVICES NAMED RUN ON WEEK-DAYS)

		a.m.	a.m.	a.m.		p.m.	p.m.	p.m.	p.m.	A p.m.	a.m.
Killybegs	... dep.	...	...	7 40	...	...	12 55	...	4 5	6 40	...
Dunkineely	... ,,	...	...	8 10	...	...	1 25	...	4 30	7 5	...
Inver	... ,,	...	...	8 26	...	...	1 41	...	4 47	7 22	...
Mountcharles	,,	...	...	8 40	...	...	1 55	...	4 59	7 35	...
Donegal	... arr.	...	...	8 55	...	...	2 10	...	5 14	7 50	...

		a.m.	a.m.	a.m.		p.m.	p.m.	p.m.	p.m.	A p.m.	C a.m.
Ballyshannon	... dep.	...	...	7 55	...	...	12 0	...	4 0	7 0	10 30
Rossnowlagh	... ,,	...	...	8 16	...	...	12 21	...	4 21	7 21	10 50
Ballintra	... ,,	...	...	8 29	...	...	12 34	...	4 34	7 34	...
Donegal	... arr.	...	...	8 55	...	...	1 0	...	4 58	8 0	...

		a.m.	a.m.	a.m.		p.m.	p.m.	p.m.	p.m.	p.m.	a.m.
Donegal	... dep.	...	...	9 2	...	...	2 13	...	5 20	...	...
Stranorlar	... arr.	...	...	9 57	...	...	3 10	...	6 13	...	...
Stranorlar	... dep.	...	8 15	9 58	...	1 15	3 15	4 55	6 15	...	...
Killygordon	... ,,	...	8 25	10 8	...	1 25	3 27	5 5	6 25	...	...
Castlefin	... arr.	...	8 35	10 20	...	1 36	3 37	5 15	6 37	...	...
Castlefin	... dep.	...	8 36	10 25	...	1 38	3 45	5 17	6 39	...	...
Strabane	... arr.	...	8 55	10 44	...	1 57	4 5	5 37	6 59	...	...

		a.m.	a.m.	a.m.		p.m.	p.m.	p.m.	p.m.	A p.m.	a.m.
Strabane	... dep.	7 35	...	11 0	...	2 50	...	6 5	7 35	...	...
Lifford	... arr.	7 36	...	11 1	...	2 51	...	6 6	7 36	...	...
Lifford	... dep.	7 41	...	11 10	...	3 0	...	6 10	7 41	...	...
Raphoe	... ,,	8 2	...	11 33	...	3 23	...	6 32	8 2	...	...
Convoy	... ,,	8 10	...	11 43	...	3 32	...	6 41	8 11	...	...
Letterkenny	arr.	8 43	...	12 20	...	4 6	...	7 5	8 35	...	...

A—Saturdays only.
B—Saturdays excepted.
C—Sundays only.

Above: CDR timetable October 1959; it lasted only until
31 December when the line closed.

Left: Railcar 12 arrives at Castlefin to pass railcar 14 and
overtake the eastbound mixed train depicted on page 87.
(*N. F. Gurley*).

The West Clare dieselised in the 1950's. Four railcars arrived in 1952 — to the final Donegal design. One of these is shown at Lahinch, when new, next to a final steam working. (*L. Hyland, IRRS*).

Another railcar pauses at Doonbeg in the rain. Note barrels of something rather stronger on the platform. (*W. McGrath Collection*).

New arrival. The first freight diesel at Ennis in September 1955. The West Clare closure was part of a widespread programme of rural railway closures in Ireland. (*W. McGrath Collection*).

There was less than a month to go when this West Clare goods crossed the River Fergus in January 1961. (*W. McGrath Collection*).

A certain amount of equipment survives. There are also a few lines, laid out to please tourists. One of the best of these is (appropriately) at Shane's Castle in Co Antrim. Apart from carrying visitors round the grounds, it acts as a base for the stock held by the North West of Ireland Railway Preservation Society. Shane's Castle Locomotive No 1 came from the Aluminium works at Larne and is dwarfed by Donegal railcar No 12 *above* and a Lough Swilly six-wheeled coach *below*. (*C. P. Friel*).

20 TODAY

everal 3ft gauge railways have been built to serve peat
ed power stations in the middle of Ireland. As a result
e total tonnage being carried over the narrow gauge is
obably higher now than it was in the heyday of the
blic lines. A train of peat for the power station waits to
oss the Grand Canal in 1968. (*J. D. C. A. Prideaux*).

IRISH NARROW GAUGE RAILWAY STATISTICS

(as at 31 December, 1911 – abstract from 1912 *Railway Year Book*)

	D	M	L	P	PT	G
allycastle	1880	16¼	4	13	2	59
astlederg & Victoria Bridge Tramway	1884	7¼	3	5	2	27
avan & Leitrim	1887	48½	9	12	12	143
ogher Valley	1887	37	7	13	7	10
ork & Muskerry	1887	18	6	19	8	60
ork, Blackrock & Passage*	1900	16	4	28	—	29
ounty Donegal Railways						
Joint Committee*	1882	125	21	56	11	304
iant's Causeway, Portrush &						
Bush Valley	1883	8	2	23	—	—
stowel & Ballybunion	1888	10	3	13	2	24
ondonderry & Lough Swilly*	1883	99½	18	49	8	274
idland Railway – Northern Counties						
Committee:						
Ballymena Cushendall & Red Bay	1875	16½ ⎱				
Ballymena & Larne	1877	31½ ⎰	12	NA	NA	NA
Portstewart Tramway	1882	1¾	3	3	1	—
chull & Skibbereen	1886	14	4	7	6	48
alee & Dingle	1891	37½	8	20	1	77
est Clare	1887	53	11	27	7	139

otes

   Parts of these lines were originally built to Irish standard gauge (date quoted is that of opening first narrow gauge
section)

  Date of opening of first section

M Mileage worked

  Number of locomotives

  Number of passenger vehicles

T Number of other passenger train vehicles

  Number of goods vehicles

he table includes a number of corrections from that originally published in 1912.

BIBLIOGRAPHY

Fayle, H. *The Narrow Gauge Railways of Ireland*, Greenlake 1946.
Flanagan, Dr P. J. *The Cavan & Leitrim Railway*, David & Charles 1966.
McGrath, W. and Rowlands, D. G. *The Dingle Train*, Kerry Arch. and Hist. Soc. 1978, 978, No 11 p
    No 11 pp 85–113.
McNeil, Dr D. G. *Ulster Tramways and Light Railways*, Belfast Museum 1956.
Newham, A. T. *The Schull & Skibbereen Tramway*, Oakwood 1964.
Newham, A. T. *The Cork & Muskerry Light Railway*, Oakwood 1968.
Newham, A. T. *The Cork, Blackrock & Passage Railway*, Oakwood 1970.
Patterson, Dr E. M. *The County Donegal Railways*, David & Charles 1962.
Patterson, Dr E. M. *The Lough Swilly Railway*, David & Charles 1964.
Patterson, Dr E. M. *The Ballycastle Railway*, David & Charles 1965.
Patterson, Dr E. M. *The Ballymena Lines*, David & Charles 1968.
Patterson, Dr E. M. *Clogher Valley Railway*, David & Charles.
Powell, A. J. and Whitehouse, P. B. *Tralee & Dingle Railway*, Locomotive Publishing Co.
Rowlands, D. G. *The Tralee & Dingle Railway*, Bradford Barton 1977.
The Cork Examiner.
The Journal of the Irish Railway Record Society.
The Railway Magazine.

ACKNOWLEDGEMENTS

One of the greatest pleasures in compiling a book such as this comes from the help willingly given by many friends and photographers. The author would like to acknowledge those photographers, companies and poets credited individually and particularly: John Smith (Lens of Sutton), Victor Goldberg, David Rowlands, Herbert Richards and the other Officers of the Irish Railway Record Society, Kenneth Clarke, John Harriso Mike Walsh, Norman Gurley, Tim Shuttlewort Brien Hilton and Walter McGrath, all of who have found, lent, printed, or copied photographs otherwise helped the task forward. My wife's ro has included not only typing and editing t manuscript, but also advice on matters bo equine and poetical.

Tailpiece. Leaving Ballybunion on the Listowel & Ballybunion. (*Leabharlann Naisiunta na hEireann*).